HOW SHALL WE BE SAVED?

Donald Freed

I0140057

BROADWAY PLAY PUBLISHING INC
New York
www.broadwayplaypublishing.com
info@broadwayplaypublishing.com

HOW SHALL WE BE SAVED?
© Copyright 2003 Donald Freed

Cover photo of Salome Jens and Mitchell Ryan by Friedman-Abeles

First published by B P P I in *Plays By Donald Freed, Volume Two* in September 2003
This edition: February 2019
I S B N: 978-0-88145-804-6

Book design: Marie Donovan
Page make-up: Adobe InDesign
Typeface: Palatino

HOW SHALL WE BE SAVED? was was first produced by Cinda Jackson at The Lost Studio in Los Angeles opening on 20 May 2002. The cast and creative contributors were:

ELEANOR ....Salome Jens
CONRAD ....Mitchell Ryan

Director.. Donald Freed
Set & lighting design ....Dan Cowen

CHARACTERS & SETTING

Eleanor, *middle-age*
Conrad, *middle-age*

Time: The Millenium
Place: Landscaped enclosure. Night.

for Patricia

(In the darkness, the sound cycle of C N N War Against Terror news. Then, ocean waves at a distance, and night insect sounds.)

(Moonlight beams up on ELEANOR. *She stands as if straining to hear. She moves D S toward the ocean, toward the waves. But the music from a dance band—far away, in and out on the sea breeze—stops her: show tunes from the great bands of the 1930s in and out.)*

*(*ELEANOR *begins to dance, with herself, across the patio, then, stops abruptly, listening again.)*

ELEANOR: Mr Stearne?

CONRAD: *(From somewhere in the foliage, after a long pause)* Good evening, Miss Eleanor.

ELEANOR: Pat upon your cue. Just the man I wanted to see….

*(*CONRAD, *after a long pause, comes into view and stands framed in the U L archway. He is in full black-tie dinner dress.)*

ELEANOR: An hour late, and looking very handsome… Moonlight—all in your shoes…

CONRAD: Mmm…

ELEANOR: Mmm…

CONRAD: Well, how are we today?

ELEANOR: *Abbastanza bene*, sir—as they say at Lake Como. Not bad. *Cosi-cosi*. Fair. *Ça va*. So-so. *Ça marche*. In short, pretty well, can't complain, *muy bien, ça peut aller*, and "sufficient unto the day is the evil thereof." —

Ha-ha-ha! …Don't run away, I've saved your bench—
I'm only pleasantly, ah, relaxed. Someone—was it you?
—sent me over a bottle of good *pinot*. I think there's
just—no? The "Flintridge Vineyards," very grand. He's
over ninety, the son's in charge, the "Old Man" lives in
the past, they say he was never the same after Ronald
Reagan slipped him the Presidential Medal of Honor.
Mm. Made him an honorary member of the "Kitchen
Cabinet." Know what that was? Mm. Of course, you
do… Sit. Please.

(Dance music from a distance)

ELEANOR: Listen! …Can that be the same orchestra?
(Hums) What? I danced with my father to that exact
arrangement—in 1958! The average age of those
musicians must be mid to late 80s. I'm serious. I was
conceived here. My family—this was our stomping
ground. So quiet—no planes tonight. *(Listens and sings)*
"Oh, I want to warn you, laddie…" Our watering hole.
And it's unchanged. Thirty years since I've been back,
and it's fixed in time… Of course you're a newcomer.
Tomorrow night I'll tell you the secret of the place. It's
haunted! Ghosts. Wait! Ha-ha, I'm a good ghost, I won't
bite. Hmm… So—so quiet. *(Pause)* I hope you don't
think I've ambushed you just because I can't sleep.
I sleep. I've slept half my life away, haven't we all?
The problem is there's no rest in sleep, today, because
"Responsibility begins in dreams." How could Yeats
have written that and not Freud. Of course, they were
both poets weren't they? Hmm. Anyway, here we are
again, by coincidence. Unless—it's you that can't sleep
and that's why you seek me out at night to talk you
down into sweet dreams. That's it—I'm better than
"Restoral", or whatever they call it. The only catch is
that a pleasant dream can turn into a nightmare—like
that.

(ELEANOR *snaps her fingers.* CONRAD *finally moves to the bench.*)

ELEANOR: It all depends on the state of your, ah, digestion. But I see you walking on the beach everyday with that old fashioned dog: you look fit; moderate, I'm sure, in all things, and sleep like a log. So it must be *kismet*—you are here—to keep me *awake*, for fear that I'll fall into a trance and, like Lady Macbeth, start to sleepwalk through the cottages plucking up memories—like roots—from the inmates, I mean the, hah, moneyed slumberers—all of whom are hanging in dreams on the back of a tiger.

CONRAD: …Mmmmm.

ELEANOR: Mmm.

(CONRAD *sits.*)

ELEANOR: Full moon… Years ago… Once upon a time, during the old Cold War—my husband sat next to, then, President Reagan, in Beverly Hills. Word of honor! Ha. After he was elected the first time, Reagan, when he came home to California, used to like to drop in and get his hair cut at an out-of-the-way little shop half hidden behind the old Beverly Wilshire Hotel where he'd gone for years along with a host of other B types to have his hair cut and, ah, restored-you didn't think that premature purple was nature, did you? Ha. Your smile tells me perhaps you were not an impassioned supporter of the Gipper—I've completely forgotten why he was sometimes called that, called himself that— "Win one for the Gipper!" A sports reference, was it? Mm… Well, after he became a great man, and the Leader of the Free World, he used to drop in for a trim, and a touch-up, for old-time's sake. So, on the day I'm referring to, my husband was there having his hair cut short, when he looked up, ha!, you see my husband had just stepped into this

particular salon many years before, quite by accident,
when he'd first come to Los Angeles and got lost in
Beverly Hills, saw this little barber shop, went in,
and being a man of some habit continued to frequent
this "tonsorial emporium," as he liked to call it, for a
number of years until the day I'm telling you about.
(She sips her wine.) So, there he was, Gerald, my spouse,
sitting as usual, blocking out the litany of dirty jokes
that his man—Tony, I think it was—always poured
into his ear, and brooding, I have no doubt, about our
dirty war in Nicaragua and whether or not it might
be time to employ the "Weapons of the Brave" —by
which he meant a hunger strike to the death—when
he chanced to open his eyes and couldn't help noting
that several muscular types with cords in their ears
were standing about the place. One in the doorway
was in leather, he said, and the other two wore blazers.
Dark wrap around sunglasses, of course. As I say, he
focused on this sinister seeming entourage, hadn't a
clue, and then, I suppose, he took in the ancient black
and white photos framed on the walls—you know,
B-movie gangster types of yesteryear, J Edgar Hoover
in all his G-Man chic, a clutch of fast-tough Mexican
boys, all of them contenders—saw all that black and
white for the first time, all inscribed to "Lou", the
squat barber/bookie from Hell's Kitchen who'd owned
the joint since the thirties—and it came to him as in a
dream that the man under the towel lying next to him,
in the next chair, had to be the President, and that the
thugs in mufti must be agents, S S! Secret Service body
guards! *(She chuckles.)* He stalked out, like a shot, and
never returned, but he told the story 'till the day he
died, wonderfully, in excruciating detail, or rather, I
did. Ha! Marvelous, isn't it? Better than a play. And
there's a kicker: Tony, our man, Gerald's barber, called
Gerald once—he was opening his own shop—and told
him that after the Gipper had finished his second term

and retired to California, that he and the First Lady
used to have a barber, and a manicurist, for her, sent
out to the mansion, that the Kitchen Cabinet had paid
for, and that not only had this service been gratis, but
that not once had the ex-President or the First Lady
ever given the barber or the manicurist a tip. Not once.
Never. Not a penny! This foretold, my husband stated,
just how dangerous Reagan's Rambo-Rocky revolution
through Rotary really would be.

*(*CONRAD *sneezes.* ELEANOR *shoots to her feet, in reaction.)*

CONRAD: Excuse me.

ELEANOR: My husband understood that Reagan was
an empty mirror, that the country saw itself reflected
in those vacant eyes, but what you never knew, or
understood, or any of the pundits, or the chattering
class, didn't have a clue—that "Dutch" Reagan was
not a simple-minded, hen-pecked, all-American hair-
cut. Dutch Reagan and Dick Nixon were slow boys at
school and sly boys at home. Spying on their fathers,
ruined in the Great Depression, wearing hand-me-
downs, nursing their envy, these punching bags
on the high school football team—Gerald knew all
this—sucking up to the New York dream-makers in
Hollywood. Dutch and Dick waiting for their chance,
secretly cultivating every jackleg fascist in their "Law
& Order", "Southern Strategy", "Silent Majority", and,
finally, "Moral Majority" crusade, until their hour
rolled round at last and the big boys at Bohemian
Grove gave Dutch and Dick their marching orders. But
the point is this: Ronald Wilson Reagan was not just a
bad B-movie actor, or a dumb sleepy cheerleader, oh,
no, long before he was senile—when he was young—
in the thirties, kissing Edward G Robinson's ass and
joining Jewish anti-fascist fronts—he was already
working undercover against the Hollywood unions
just as he later spied for the F B I. Ronald Resentment

always knew that the Jews and the rest of the Educated
Class would look down their noses at him and smile
superciliously until he wiped the smirk off their face.
But what my husband, Gerry, knew was…that the
American People are so lost, so lonely, so scared that
Reagan's chemistry of goofy geniality, his crackpot
world-view, the barely buried burning envy and
resentment; his sense of failure—remember he told the
Press that the only Blacklist in Hollywood was against
him! And his ilk of put-upon patriots. So he was a
winner with the soul of a loser and the public saw
through the pancake makeup and the hair dye and ice-
cream suits, saw through into the empty desert of his
soul, saw the chintz curtains, the Philco radio on the
fritz, the linoleum, the drunk out-of-work father—I'm
not talking about the racists and the rich who always
cast Dutch, the department store dummy, to star in
their own Kitchen Kabinet Kitsch—that's "K-K-K"—
No, I'm talking about Joe and Josifina Sixpack, the
American working class that believed they were the
"Middle Class," and who followed the Gipper down
the field and over the cliff. The terrified white trash
who knew that he was one of their own who'd won a
beauty contest, and they wanted a moment of beauty
and ease, too…. Those frantic fanatic crowds were all
screaming only one thing—out of the black orifice of
their yelling— "How shall we be saved?!"…And all
his cue card answers added up to "Follow me to the
City on the Hill, to New Jerusalem, and I will give you
rest—and Justice, because I've had it up to my keister
with these longhairs, and these liquor store minorities,
these bleeding hearts." He didn't spell it out, but the
little people huddled underneath the Golden Arches
understood *him* even as he knew *them*…"How shall
we be saved?" *(She sings part of* Amazing Grace.*)* You
know, Mr Stearne, at least that Max-Factored bundle of
secrets and his lost electorate knew, behind the friendly

fascism, under the shit-kicking small talk and lies, that they were—lost, damned, road-kill on the Information Highway that had to be saved! And the Establishment, our class, not only had no eyes for these Main Street wanderers but our crowd despised them—their clothes and their culture—because we were already and had long since been "saved", and the editorial page of *The New York Times* was our gospel... *(Pause)* Of course there were exceptions. Me, myself. My husband—and, I've no doubt, you, yourself.... Anyway, naturally, the Gipper and the First Dame were shameless. Never gave a working barber or manicurist a nickel. Somehow, he said, my husband, that told it all. Not a penny...that tore it, he said—my husband...You sure you won't try my *pinot*? Not a penny, not a dime, not a *sou*, not a *kopeck*. It gave him the "reds", he said, my husband. "Reds" means intense irritation, for "red-ass" —ha! Yes, in other words, Ronald Reagan gave him the red ass—that's what Gerald meant by "reds" —in that sense, but, of course, he was only too aware of other meanings, but in this case "reds" meant the opposite of "blues". The Reds and the Blues. Gerald was a southern boy from Mississippi. Everybody knows the blues—"Everybody's got the blues/blues all in my plate..."—that's the kind of thing they used to sing down there. "Woke up dis mawnin', blues all in my plate"...But up here in the North, down in Southern California, people are mainly ignorant of this lesser or archaic or regional reading of "reds"... *(Pause)* Rain? Maybe. Tomorrow... Your flight?

CONRAD: What's that?

ELEANOR: What time is your flight?

CONRAD: ...I'm not sure.

ELEANOR: You're not?

CONRAD: Because, uh...

ELEANOR: There's a problem....

CONRAD: I'm not sure.

ELEANOR: Ahh...These hydrangeas, they, ah, have to be
watered every day. Every day. Every night...Moon's
down. "The moon is down, and she goes down at—"
What?... Macbeth. Lady Macbeth, a pundit once called
me that, on one of these "T V Specials" of, ah, long-
headed Beltway bozos. "Lady Macbeth"—but it didn't
catch on, didn't stick…. Anyway, Ronald Reagan gave
us the reds, and he gave us the blues. The blues—not
to be confused with depression, "clinical depression,"
as it's now called. The blues are not, ah, there's nothing
"clinical" about the blues, or reds, either, for that
matter. They're right out there in the world! And the
one causes the other. The reds lead to the blues, if what
it is that's giving you the reds is beyond your ability
to do anything about the situation. And the blues will
produce an extreme case of the reds as soon as you
do decide to do something about your condition. His
hemorrhoids, my husband's, were not caused because
he sat and wrote six hours a day, they were caused
by Dutch Reagan and his Kitchen Cabinet—*they* gave
him the reds, it was not "the writer's disease." They
gave *him* the reds and *me* the blues. So, he went to
Nicaragua, and I stayed home… (*She looks out into
the past.*) *No esta olvidado*…"Here's looking at you,
kid." Dead soldier… Moon's up, again…I'd had the
blues all my life, except the concept was foreign to
me—not having been Mississippi born—so Dr Brown
and mother called it depression, or, later, "clinical
depression" —after Dr Brown, a staunch Reagan hard-
liner, had drunk himself to death and been replaced by
Dr Chester—this was when Reagan was first Governor,
and we thought he was a joke, 'till we found out who
laughed last. Dr Chester was not a drunk, he was a
liberal, and he prescribed repeated doses of Penis

Erectus—not to Mother, of course—and it has to be
said that he did chase the blues away—for a while….
After Dr Chester came Miriam Marcus and it was Dr
Marcus who told me, first, about the blues and how
"We suffer as the sparks fly upwards." God love her,
it was 1968 by this time and I had confronted Father,
over the war and, ah, other things, Mother was dead—
"by her own hand," as they used to say in Trollope's
novels—and I'd met the hero of "The Free Speech
Movement" at Stanford. I say hero, because Gerald
was no guerilla with tenure spraying Marxist rhetoric
over the heads of a generation of onion-skinned
adolescents—he was not one of your toughs of the
tender Left dining out on the Vietnamese people—no!
Gerald was—well, you heard him speak, you said,
at Harvard; you've read his books, you know the
story. When he quit Stanford in '68 the dye was cast.
I had to choose as well. I had my inheritance from
Grandmother. Gerald had some money. He said to me,
quoting from Trollope, "I love you, my own darling
girl, more than all the world besides"…"More than all
the world besides."…I suppose it was that rich mixture
of Marx and Trollope that made me come, ah, to the
conclusion that this was the revolutionist for me.

(Pause. CONRAD *looks at his watch.)*

ELEANOR: Conrad, would you like—*in vino*, et cetera—
you drink hardly at all—of course, we never did, in
those days, especially marijuana. You had informers
and provocateurs everywhere—talk about Eastern
Europe, America is informers from sea to shining sea…
Gerald taught me: the trick was to resist paranoia
and infantile trust, equally, so that while you might
be a fool for the Revolution, you were not one for the
State. People don't talk like that any more, do they?
You probably never did—but before I drive you away
absolutely, Comrade, Conrad, let me just make my

point: Gerald was a revolutionist—am I losing you?
Hmm—put it this way: a revolutionist is, actually, a
rebel. A "rebel with limits," a Free Lance, a minority
of one with, ah, "judicious indignation," according
to Erik Erikson. I always liked that, but, then, I may
be biased, my psychoanalyst had been a student of
Erikson's. She used to refer to a cure as a "remnant of
judicious indignation." One, ha, day I asked her—this
was 1969—if "judicious indignation" did or did not
mean buying guns for the I R A or the Black Panther
Party? And her reply was, predictably, "What do you
think?"...Well, I did think I knew what she meant,
then—but, now, I'm no longer certain. Not so sure, at
any rate...not really certain at all... Because, at that
time, though violence and war were raging around us,
I had not, personally, been affected, directly affected,
by any violence personally—in person.

(CONRAD *seems to be in pain.*)

ELEANOR: You must be cold. It's terrible to be talked to
death. Shall I let you go?

CONRAD: My foot keeps going to sleep.

ELEANOR: You're a good sport, Conrad.

CONRAD: Yes and no.

ELEANOR: You are! —Here, give me your paw.

(CONRAD *complies, in excruciating slow motion.* ELEANOR
opens his fist and reads his palm.)

ELEANOR: Let's walk. That's it. Step, step—I like your
limp. Ha! Put your hand out, you know, begging.
Excellent! *(She mimes a scene with him.)* You're to the
manner born. Stand this way—bravo! —And I'll
stand here, holding up a big sign: "He will dance for
money?" *(Imitating Mae West)* "Are those handcuffs in
your pocket, Mr Stearne—or are you just glad to see
me?"

CONRAD: *(Laughing)* Mmm—tickling me.

ELEANOR: Just joking.

CONRAD: It's only my gate key. Gate key.

ELEANOR: …You may sit, now, sir. Sit. Well done. Better? Yes. Little by little…

CONRAD: …Thank you. That was a good laugh, that was fun.

ELEANOR: Oh, yes. You're a good soul and you'll know better, next time, not to ask a woman of a certain rage, stopping at the most expensive hotel in the world—ha-ha! —not to ask her, in the moonlight, "How are we *today*?" A-ha, ha! …After my father dropped dead, my attitude toward violence changed. It changed, again, after the police and the F B I executed that beautiful Black Panther, Fred Hampton—I knew him, quite well—and, again, with my daughter—you don't know about that—and then, finally, with Gerald, when he left for Nicaragua…. Can I sit over here, my shoulder's a little stiff. That's good…. Actually, my father was a homicide not a suicide. I came home from Stanford and went up to Fairfield and caught him after breakfast before he set out for Manhattan. You sure you want to hear this—how I murdered my father? Mm. You see? You're a very good soul…. So I said, "Daddy," I said, "You know that I know that you know that I know that you know. But," I continued, "no one else will ever know except Dr Marcus, and she will always protect the privilege. *Always!*" …He just looked at me. He was in his dressing gown. I felt for him—in a way. Am I frightening you? …He turned around and went upstairs. I stood where I was. I waited—listening. With my back to the empty fireplace. Complete silence. Where were Sally and the servants? Hmm. Silence. I would've heard him on the telephone, or the commode flushing. Nothing. I waited about ten minutes, then

I left, flew on to Washington for the March on the Pentagon. Sally found him upstairs in his bedroom, just after I left, dead. Heart…I killed him. He did his part by dying. I killed, he died. No violence, you see? None. Magic. Voodoo. He had violated the taboo—he had to die. But I had violated the taboo, too, by telling, so I had to die, too, except that I had a way out because I was dead already—and had been since I was eleven years old—no one could kill me again, but Daddy was still kicking so he had to die…. So, then he was dead, and I was "undead" —not alive, but no longer dead. They wired me in Washington and I tried to make love all night to Gerald, in Saint John's Cathedral—where we were sleeping with the San Francisco contingent— but it was no good. The killing of my father was good. And me being undead was certainly a plus. But I needed something more than black magic—I needed a Black Panther to rape me in Chicago, to start the ball rolling, and that's exactly what happened. To be continued? —No? Hmm, you're more than a good sport, you are in Mr Trollope's phrase, a "Lad of Wax."…Mmm…Conrad…

CONRAD: Yes.

ELEANOR: I have to ask you to do something….

CONRAD: Yes.

ELEANOR: I'm so sorry….

CONRAD: What?

ELEANOR: It's humiliating, really…

CONRAD: What?

ELEANOR: …You see that, ah, spider?

CONRAD: …Where?

ELEANOR: Don't move…there.

CONRAD: Oh.

ELEANOR: …Could you…

CONRAD: I'll kill it.

ELEANOR: No!

CONRAD: Why not?

ELEANOR: Could you just, ah, move it?

CONRAD: Just step on it.

ELEANOR: No. Please. I beg you.

CONRAD: What's the problem?

ELEANOR: Would you just move it away—with your handkerchief?

CONRAD: No, ma'am.

ELEANOR: I see.

CONRAD: …What's the problem?

ELEANOR: …There's a napkin, there, on the table.

CONRAD: …Alright… *(He brushes the spider away.)* No problem. We're safe and sound.

ELEANOR: Yes…Thank you. *(She stretches out at his feet. Music, again, on the breeze.)* … "And down by the shore, an orchestra's playing…" That was how they lived then. Cigarettes, martinis, Bay Rum, Brooks Brothers, white bucks, black servants, black bucks, white lies…This was their resort and their rehab; their retreat and their ranch and their redoubt… This was years ago—on the "American Plan" —four meals a day—all you could eat—the "American Plan"… *(Speaks the words)* "Oh, yes, let them begin the beguine, make them play"… *(Silence, then she climbs back to the present.)* Where were we? Ah—February 1968, my father. *(She stares out remembering.)* Then came the Ides of March. This is when we had our nervous breakdown. I say "we" because on March 1, Robert McNamara finally gave up on Vietnam and quit the Pentagon; March 15,

the Wall Street "Wisemen" told the President that the
war was lost; March 31, the President resigned, or the
same thing; April 4, Martin Luther King was executed
and the cities went up in fire; June 6, Bobby Kennedy
was gunned down and, as I say, the country went
into a *crise de nerfs*—like Germany before, like Chile
three years later…. So by August, it was all sex and
violence and then I was raped and then the F B I and
Chicago police slaughtered Fred Hampton—but don't
misunderstand—the thug that set up Mr Hampton and
had me on a church altar was a police agent, not an
authentic Panther, but even if he had been—well, the
Panthers were human and they were young—don't
look so stricken, sir.

(CONRAD *stands, removes his jacket, folds it neatly.*)

ELEANOR: These same "black cats" were, all in all, in
every way morally superior not only to my father but
to those same Wise Men who had driven the country
mad and who would go on through the torture
chambers of Chile until Ronald Reagan invaded
Grenada and mined the waters of Nicaragua and killed
my husband at Ilipongo… (*She stands and acts out her
glorious memory of life and love.*) I want you to picture
Black Panther Chairman Fred Hampton, "Chairman
Fred," on Calumet Avenue in the dead of the Chicago
winter—organizing walking wounded ex-cons, and
limousine liberals, and refugees from suburbia, like
me—at six in the A M—to feed black and brown and
hungry white kids, to "suffer the little children"—and
for a few minutes God was alive in America—until the
clock struck thirteen. (*She rocks back and forth. The waves
pound.*) Ahh…Conrad, I tell you what. It will positively
help to wake up your feet.

CONRAD: What?

ELEANOR: To dance. Shall we? Dance or die!

CONRAD: No thanks.

ELEANOR: Doctor's orders. Gershwin. No one's watching. "Dance like no one's watching" —Satchel Page said—and "Love like you've never been hurt."

CONRAD: I don't dance, actually.

ELEANOR: Virtually, then. A virtual foxtrot. "Someone to watch over me…"

CONRAD: …I can't!

(ELEANOR dances by herself, singing a verse.)

ELEANOR: …That's how the foxes trotted in daddy's day. *(Dances another step)* At the dances in Daddyland. —In the Fatherland. *(Silence)* I am not clinging to the past, Mr Stearne, not looking backward, it's just that, ah, "Objects in mirror are closer than they appear" — and I know as intimately as you that the past is dead, it doesn't exist, and, therefore—we are free. *The 1960s was a war. We lost. That's all! (Pause)* So we're free. Free and alone and, ah, condemned to choose… Have you made you choice, Conrad? Is tonight the night?… Did you just wink at me—or is that a tic? *(Pause)* "He hears no music"… Seriously, Conrad—don't you have some favorite? Some song? *Something…*

(CONRAD searches for a full minute, through his memory. ELEANOR tries to give moral support. Finally:)

CONRAD: "Fight on for U S C… Fight on to victory!"

ELEANOR: Ah-hah, a regular Trojan… So am I. *(She lifts the wine bottle.)* "Lights in our hands, old music on our lips, Wild honey and the East, and loveliness." … So, I was raped by the agent, O'Neil, and I should've killed him because, unlike my father, he, O'Neil, was not going to drop dead for fear of exposure. Because father, unlike O'Neil, had everything to lose, because when a man like my father is, ah, exposed he ceases, at one stroke, being a high Republican Party mover and shaker; he is no longer a prominent Episcopal *layman*; nor the applauded *philanthropist* at the speakers' table; not an American patriot, a Christian gentleman, a husband, a father, a *man!* —no, when the Word is spoken even in the sanctity of the psychotherapist's office, that Word can never be unsaid and father must die. *Taboo!* ...Fred Hampton was a young hero; the rapist, O'Neil, was a creature of the Government; Daddy, was, ah, a "pillar of society"; they all died violently; and Mother...I was close to each one of them; it could have easily been me (they found a revolver in Daddy's briefcase that day), but I lived through that summer of '68—and they didn't—and I lived through Chile and Nicaragua—and my husband did not—my daughter...that's another story (mmm, excuse me). But I did, more or less, live, undead until this moonlit hour.... Listen, the tide's coming in-and in and in—like a revenant, an unlaid ghost. A ghost. Unlaid.

(Silence. CONRAD *wipes his lip.)*

ELEANOR: Now, today, there are rape hotels in the center of Europe. Rape is all the rage, again, a hundred years and more after my heroic ancestor Mrs Pankhurst set the House of Parliament in flames. O, Mrs Pankhurst: behold the Age of Aquarius, the Age of Progress! O Mother Pankhurst, Men have given Women the franchise, the vote, birth control, financial control; permission to work, to write, to abort, to fight, to love, to lust, to be Prime Ministers and President. This, I say, is Progress! Rest in peace, Mrs Pankhurst— Rest! ...There is, however, one tiny catch: men are raping woman on a scale unequaled in the long, weary increment since Genesis—where, as we now know, Adam, Jehovah, and the snake, the serpent, gang-banged Eve. That's your first modern date rape, there's your trinity of lies and rape—born out of *his* rib, was she? Ha! Even in the moonlight

you're blushing, Conrad, and it does you great credit.
(She assumes the role of a teacher.) This is not revision,
this is reality. Let us consider these ur-gangbangers.
Long-bearded Jehovah fashioned Adam out of clay in
his own image and vice-a-versa, then like the sublime
cosmic artist that He was—he with a capital "H" —He
took it into his matted, dreadlocked, gray-bearded
head to rip a woman out of Adam's rib cage. *Aaarghhh!*
Shh, not too loud. Ripped her out. This was your first
caesarian section, and handed her over to the serpent,
who in his slimy turn, passed the bitch on to Adam,
himself, for sloppy thirds, who threw the tramp into
the street, or rather the desert, where she was renamed
"Original Sin" and danced topless at the Desert Inn.
(She dances.) This is Western Civilization! Outside the
house it's rape, inside it's the holy trinity. *(Sings)* "Just
like a silver dollar goes from hand to hand/ a woman
goes from man to man…" O Mrs Pankhurst, Mother
mine, seeist thou how this our twentieth century, at
millennium ending, your daughters have climbed up
out of the gutters of Ur—behold the New Woman—out
of the loins of Hedda and Nora and Anna and Emma
and Scarlet, out of their birth pangs, Mrs Pankhurst,
has been born this new woman! The future stretches
out flat and free; there are no whores hitching on the
Information Highway that leads to New Jerusalem—O,
Mother, I cannot deny that here, there, everywhere
from Lake Como to the East End of London—
women are still prey to the old Adam—but not in the
mittlewelt of that "Gated Community" we call the
future. There, Mrs P, we have achieved the "Final
Solution" *(Nazi accent)* to the historical problem we
call rape. And that solution is—Rape Without Women!
Economic rape, environmental rape, cultural, political,
ethnic rape—without women, without sex, without
the need of the phallus, therefore (altogether, girls!) no
more phallus envy in the Gated Community, where

the family reigns supreme, and rape is a remnant
of a distant atavistic age. You lift your eyebrow, Mr
Stearne, you judge that I exaggerate—slightly? I would
not be guilty of that, Mr Stearne, Conrad, it would
not be fair to Mrs. Pankhurst, to Mrs Sanger, to Carrie
Nation, herself. I do not say that behind every gate a
beloved father, an uncle, a trusted friend, a husband,
or even a stranger—a perfect stranger—is not liable at
any moment to fall upon the daughters of the house.
(She crosses behind his bench.) It is now as it was in the
Garden when they designated Eve the victim and the
vessel of evil, death and Original Sin—for which our
Lord was crucified to pay the World's ransom—no,
Conrad, I do not asseverate that every woman, any
woman, is not actually raped, repeatedly, in all the
worlds—third, second, and first—I do not say that.
They are. They will be. My elementary point is that
in the gated world we have a universe of invisible
rape and abuse: In Europe we call this new order the
"Belgian Syndrome", and the "French Syndrome",
and the "Barcelona Syndrome", and, here, at home,
we call it the "Boulder Syndrome". And men, too,
just like you, in our, ah "penal" system—which the
guards and inmates, alike, call the "Soulbreaker", —
the largest system in the world, where I, once upon
a time, almost.... Well, that's it: rape is the name of
the game in Central Europe, and on the internet Jon
Benet Ramsey and a generation of nymphets will
dance forever on the stage of the unconscious—so rape
as we knew it is changed and changing—gone with
the wind—and the day is nigh, O Mother Pankhurst,
when the daughters of Eden will no longer be victims
by definition. The generic descendants of Baroness
Thatcher will have their very own big bombs, their
own lasers, their own death squads, and men will not
want to rape them—nooo! —And these new women
will no longer need or want the men that they married

when they were young, won't need to be inseminated by them because in the gated world there are gene-banks to draw from, and poor breed-women to carry the fetal supermen to term.

(Dance music, ELEANOR *sways.)*

ELEANOR: That's the story, Mr Stearne: men without women, women without men. Eve fallen and Christ crucified—no more. Original Sin and Resurrection are a back number, yesterday's headline. Because, you see, "The Gated Community" is the, ah, cortex of the Superpower, the cerebellum, and it is not only gated it is wired! And this cortex is hidden right under Uncle Sam's top hat. In fact, the Gated City is the "post-modern", "deconstructed", "semiotic", "virtual", "City on the Hill" —you won't find this Utopia on any map because it's nowhere and everywhere like atomic ash, like the New World Order! Oh, yes, my friend, the New World Order is upon us. It's inside us. My father will rise from his sealed cryogenic container and be reunited with Jon Benet Ramsey in that gated little Gated City on the Hill. For "That is how we live now, Sir!" Check it out—on Amazon-dot-com.

*(*ELEANOR *pants for breath.* CONRAD *shifts in pain.)*

ELEANOR: You're retiring? They haven't locked the gate yet—shall we leave the grounds? There's a riptide rising. Shall we? Before the waves close over our heads? Homeless together? We can get out. I know the password. So do you. The password is— "Yes."

*(*CONRAD *lifts his leg.)*

ELEANOR: —Oh, no, your poor foot's fallen asleep, again. We're raising the dead, here. Mm, it could be worse. It's a terrible fate to be talked to death, but, then, you did make inquiries as to my health— "How are we *today*", is how I recall your phrasing that delightful question. And I am limiting my response precisely to today, and tonight of course, with, I assure you, no thought for the morrow, since the night, though no longer young, is not yet done—is it? The last nocturnal act is still to be played out—or you and I would not be here—in our assigned places. "Places for Act Three, please—Act Three beginners, please..." Hmm. There's just a jot more about me that you need to know and then it'll be your turn.

CONRAD: *(Groans)* Mmm.

ELEANOR: Did you wink?

(CONRAD loosens his tie.)

ELEANOR: I have to go, now. That's what you want— what? ...Shall I go, now? ...Then I'll go—and never look back.

(ELEANOR is moving. CONRAD gives a great sneeze, in pain.)

ELEANOR: *(Continuing)* God bless you!

CONRAD: Excuse me.

ELEANOR: Bless you.

CONRAD: Thank you.

ELEANOR: *(Sings)* "Bless em all, bless em all, the long and the short and the tall..." *(Offering a napkin as she stands over him)* You know what they say about sneezing?... Have you had your shots?

CONRAD: *(Pause, mopping his face)* Have you?

ELEANOR: There's a look in your eye...I can't quite, ah, read you. You are not "Government," as we used to say—that is, you are not here to spy on me. That I'm sure of. Hah, the last turnover of Government dossiers to my attorney concluded with the unforgettable caveat, "Subject is now middle-aged and no longer considered dangerous." Close quotes. Do you love it? Are you too warm? Anyway, the C I A or M I 5 would never pay the rates of this pleasuredome…. Ummm, that's why I say that I believe your interest in me is genuine, and then, too, you are one of the most impressive listeners I have ever encountered. And I've looked. Yes. I've been looking—for several perfect things…one of them being a perfect listener. Perhaps, between us, we exhaust all known modes of verbal, ah, intercourse possible between *Homo sapiens*. I'd like to say a word or two about *Homo sapiens*, but first I'll just finish my unexpurgated saga. I cannot resist your riveting attention; but, truthfully, what more is there to say? I will sum up my love-life for you thusly: I have lived with and been loved by a Fascist, and a Communist and, in each case, I took out the garbage! —Your low laugh is a pleasure to me, Mr Stearne. Conrad. So much for my lovelife. What else? Family? Not the Jukes not the Kallikaks can hold a candle to the extended sampling-error of my family tree. I dare say no more until we have vetted, between us, the issue of *Homo sapiens*. My father you know—*Homo Amerikanus*, now extinct—my husband you can still see smiling on baby boomer's fading tee-shirts…. My children… have been sold into Egypt…And that, I believe at long last, is enough about me…"Subject is now middle-aged and no longer considered dangerous"… Are you winking—or weeping?

(CONRAD *rocks slowly, in pain.* ELEANOR *watches, then draws on her final reserves.*)

ELEANOR: The truth is you don't know anymore about who you are than your great grandfather and his pals in Paleolithic times! All you know is (are you ready for it?!) we are capable of breeding with Neanderthal Man! *(She begins to lash him to life with her voice.)* So all hail to thee, Cro-Magnon man, your knuckles do not graze the ground!

(CONRAD *staggers up, stamping his foot.*)

ELEANOR: That's it, Conrad, stand up—*Ecce Homo!*—
behold the man—*Homo erectus!* —The thing itself—
now, straighten up, that's it, the end of the line,
Robert Redford! Stamp! Stamp! Stamp! *Homo erectus*
becomes *Homo sapiens* and there is no Neanderthal in
the woodpile! We are the King and the Duke! We are
Homo sapiens sapiens! But that does not mean that we
are Human Beings. No, sir. It means that we are the
creatures who have *called* ourselves human beings—
too soon…. So, you see, I do, at least, know your type,
and ah, your "family" —which makes us—what? —
collateral cousins, co-conspirators, man and wife?

(CONRAD *is grunting in pain, stamping—dangerous.*)

ELEANOR: Don't look like that—there's only one word
you can get in edgewise around here and that's "Yes"!

(CONRAD *gropes toward the U S arch.* ELEANOR *cuts him
off, her voice drilling through his rising moans.*)

ELEANOR: This is my garden, sir, here, right here,
where once the Jesuits tortured and "converted" the
Indians to the one "True Faith". So get out if you can—
because this is the endgame!

(ELEANOR *bars the arch with her body.* CONRAD *crawls
toward her. She drives at him.*)

ELEANOR: Stand up, goddamit! You think I've surfaced
after all these years—as the leader of some Amazonian
Apparat—to convert you to the Cause, the Crusade,
that I hasten to tell you is simply—to save the world!
Because the world has been wrecked on our watch—
And there is a shit-storm coming! —from which we
need to be saved—and that it's time for an accounting,
if we intend to call ourselves Homo sapiens, let alone
"Human Beings"!

(ELEANOR *has driven* CONRAD *back D S—now with a
roar of anguish he turns on her; lurches to her, fists raised;*

*roaring. She stands open—roaring back! He does not kill
her. They are frozen. Then, he halts to the U S cottage wall,
and subsides.)*

ELEANOR: *(Softly)* Gesundheit!

CONRAD: *(Choked)* Forgive me!

(ELEANOR crosses up to CONRAD, leans against the wall.)

ELEANOR: …Do you need the facility?

*(CONRAD wanders back to sit near his bench, touching
roses, seeing the moon, coming back to life.)*

ELEANOR: I just have to tell you, straight from the
shoulder, that, concerning "Revolution", which along
with "Terrorism", has become the cheapest word
in any language, next to "God" —that no one living
knows what "Revolution" means, or rather, everybody
does—"The first shall be the last, and the last shall
be the first"—except that doesn't mean anything in
the light of so-called human nature, which we are
assured is red in fang and claw. This is where Marx
lost his way, like Saint Paul before him, and predicted
the "End of History". The End of History and the
"Withering Away of the State" is as much hot air as the
"Transubstantiation of Souls" and the resurrection of
our vile bodies at the last trump…. No, Mr Stearne, I'm
afraid that we will "wither away" long before the State.
And yet…there is the moment of revolution and it is
real! A home-truth as real as the moment of solidarity,
or catharsis, or epiphany, or orgasm! *(Singing softly)*
"Arise ye prisoners of starvation…"

*(ELEANOR sits. Silence. Both CONRAD and ELEANOR are
spent.)*

ELEANOR: No one's coming…Revolution is just another
religion, and so the Revolutionary cries out, "What is
to be done?" just as Judeo-Christian Man cried out,
"How shall we be saved?" The answer after millennia

of slaughter has to be "*We don't know!*" All we know
is that Father Time killed Mother Nature at the corner
of Tigress and Euphrates six thousand years ago. *(She
rises, panting with a rage to live.)* Western Civilization!
The rise of the city; writing; laws; science—and
the world-historical defeat of women! Western
Civilization has driven us berserk! *(From behind, she
takes a stranglehold on him.)* But it has to stop! My
husband told me and I tell you—that "Shame is the
only revolutionary emotion" —and it is shame that
stays my hand now—and it is shame that saves your
life. *(She pulls back.)* Forgive me, Mr Stearne... Nothing
personal... But you take my point?... Nothing lasts,
Conrad. Nothing lasts: not in church, or the theatre, or
on the barricades—or in the bed.

(The sound of waves rises.)

ELEANOR: The moment of sex, like the moment of
revolution, fills up the world. Orgasm makes us into
human beings—but just for an instant...then there's
the rest of the night, and the balance of our lives. Then
the shame comes back—and Shame's idiot brother
Guilt—and cowards that we are, we begin, again,
our endless search for enemies. Just as if we weren't
all dying together, as if our *common* enemy weren't
waiting there is the shadows—disguised as Room
Service... *(She stops and kneels at his feet.)* Don't get up...
this has to stop. Now. You're pale. We're both panting.
I can almost hear your mind racing around in circles
like a rat. Thinking that there just might be one other
possibility, and that is—I've been telling you tales and
will go on for a hundred and one nights or until we
die, whichever comes sooner, to keep you from killing
me, and by that I mean leaving me....

CONRAD: *(He tries to rise, a strangled cry—)* Wait—wait!

ELEANOR: Animal pity, Mr Stearne! Animal pity! I'm at your feet like a Trollope novel—I'm the trollop at your feet. I kiss your hand—yes, don't pull away, there's no need to be ashamed of suffering—I kiss your opposing thumbs, that make us almost sapiens—I suck them…I kiss your eyes—that've seen it all—I bless your patient ears—I kiss your thin Caucasian lips—thin as an orangutan's, "the old man of the forest"—your tongue, your forked tongue, mm, mine, my long, lying tongue…. Ah, now, your Adam's apple, yes, there, where my fruit has stuck in your throat since pre-lapsarian times, in a garden akin to this, here, tonight—your pumping heart—your ribs, hah, from whence I was born, back then when men were men and could and did give birth, and not just out of their head—wait! —Don't run away—let me caress your legs, your thighs with their big muscles that are tensed to spring, for flight or fight, depending on whether you decide I'm a lady or a tiger—Buttocks! Tight and hard so that you can turn on a dime—now, the knees, your powerful Neanderthal knees to which the women of the world have been clinging for six thousand years begging for mercy—pity—love—human solidarity—no, let me finish! —Your feet, finally your feet, like mine, bruised and sore—your sore foot, your poor foot, I do not lick your boots, I kiss your wandering feet, as you will kiss mine—Shall I go on and start over from the ground up—

(CONRAD *stands.*)

ELEANOR: —or you could lower yourself down to my level, to ground level—these stones are cold and clean but underneath there's wet black earth…and under the earth are the Priests and the Indians—Fred Hampton, and Father—Mother, and Gerald—and my poor Betsy—in the quick black earth…

(ELEANOR sinks down. CONRAD pants over her; then, slowly, he lifts her to her knees.)

CONRAD: *(Softly)* Wait. *(He lifts her to her feet.)* I could kill you.

ELEANOR: You know who I am—and you will tell me who you are.... One Flesh... One Animal...I give you permission to be.... You give me permission to be.... But watch out—they're wrong, again—*I-am-still-dangerous*...

(Dance music up. Slowly, CONRAD and ELEANOR begin to dance gracefully in the fading moonlight.)

END OF PLAY

www.ingramcontent.com/pod-product-compliance
Lightning Source LLC
Chambersburg PA
CBHW070037110426
42741CB00035B/2802